Discover Dogs

by Amanda Trane

© 2017 by Amanda Trane
ISBN: 9781532402593
eISBN: 9781532402609
Images licensed from Fotolia.com
All rights reserved.
No portion of this book may be reproduced
without express permission of the publisher.
First Edition
Published in the United States by
Xist Publishing
www.xistpublishing.com
PO Box 61593 Irvine, CA 92602

The world is full of dogs. Some dogs make great pets. This pug wants to go on a walk.

Dogs come in many sizes.
A Chihuahua is a small dog with a big bark.

This is a Pomeranian.
A Pomeranian is small enough to fit inside a purse.

This Rottweiler is a big dog. She is tall enough to grab food off of the table.

All dogs have hair or fur. This Springer Spaniel has long, wavy fur.

This Poodle had his fur cut to look fancy. It takes many hours to brush a poodle.

14

This is a Labradoodle.
She has curly fur.

Some dogs have very short hair. This Pit Bull has soft, short hair.

A Bernese Mountain Dog needs long fur to keep warm in the snow.

Some dogs have jobs.
This is a German Shepherd.
You may see a German Shepherd working with the military.

21

This bloodhound has a big job. He can find people using only his nose.

Some dogs work to protect their homes. This Doberman Pinscher might scare people away.

25

Some dogs do not work at all. This is a lazy bulldog.

Most dogs can be trained to be good pets. This Labrador Retriever would be a great pet.

This Yorkshire Terrier would be a good pet for someone who likes to take short walks.

When you see a dog, look at their fur and their size. Watch the dogs you see to find out if they have jobs or if they are pets. The world is full of dogs!

33

www.ingramcontent.com/pod-product-compliance
Lightning Source LLC
LaVergne TN
LVHW010020070426
835507LV00001B/23